Turning to God to Get Through Grief

Edited by Linus Mundy

Abbey Press

St. Meinrad, IN 47577

Text © 2004 Abbey Press
Published by One Caring Place
Abbey Press
St. Meinrad, Indiana 47577

ISBN 978-0-87029-379-5

Printed in the United States of America

Introduction

❧

"It will take a miracle for me to get through this," someone once told me after the loss of someone very dear. The truth is, that's what it takes for any of us to survive, isn't it? Sometimes only God can get us through.

This small book is all about the ways God "gets us through" the hardest of times; how we miraculously can survive the loss of someone very near and dear to us.

The five short chapters that make up this book first appeared (and still appear) as "CareNotes"—small Abbey Press publications that have brought help and hope to millions upon millions of readers.

It is our hope that *Turning to God to Get Through Grief* will provide the same generous amounts of help and hope to you, dear reader. And maybe the beginnings of a miracle.

—Linus Mundy, Editor

Contents

∾

CHAPTER I

Walking With God Through Grief and Loss

∾

By Joyce Rupp, O.S.M.

One of the most pain-filled letters I ever received was from a young mother whose firstborn child had died. She was overwhelmed with the depth of this loss. All her plans and hopes and dreams came crashing down around her, and she couldn't fathom how she could ever find joy in life again.

The letter poured out her anguish and despair. She felt, she said, as if God had abandoned her at a time when she most needed this Loving Presence. She *even thought* of taking her life, so deep was her desolation.

As I read her letter, I sensed a deep desire in her to walk with God even though she found no comfort when she tried to pray. Over and over she pleaded for some insight, some direction, on how to relate to God during her time of darkness.

The painful emotions described in that letter haunt many human hearts caught up in grief and loss. The negative feelings we have during such times are natural. Yet they bewilder us because we do not expect or accept them as a part of the experience. We want to rid ourselves of the unpleasant feelings as quickly as possible, but grief takes time. We must recognize our feelings of loss and learn to live with them for a time as best we can.

Working your way through | Faith questions naturally arise during these agonizing times: How can I walk with God when God seems to have forgotten all about me? How can I pray when I hurt so much? What do I do when the ways that I used to pray don't work for me? When we feel engulfed by such questions, there are some helps to which we can turn.

❧ *Picture God on your side.* The way we picture God has much to do with the way we walk with God during our time of loss. It is helpful to picture God as being on our side rather than against us or responsible for our suffering.

Harold Kushner tells us in *When Bad Things Happen to Good People* that God does not send suffering to us; rather, suffering and loss are a result of the human condition.

Picturing God as One who is on our side is a strong biblical image. God will never abandon us or forget us. God has great compassion for us, yearning for our peace and joy. Many writers see God as suffering with us, walking the road of our grief, having infinite concern for us.

As we pray during our time of grief, we can picture God sitting by our side, looking upon us with much love, or walking with us and listening to our story of sorrow.

༚ *Trust in God's nearness and goodness.* When we are grieving a significant loss, our world can seem bleak and dark. We may feel that God does not care or doubt that God even exists. Grief is a time to trust that God is very close, even though our feelings say otherwise.

When we are depressed and all we can think about is our sadness, it helps to call on our good memories. We recall people and events that have brought us happiness. These memories assure us that God

God is not only the God of the sufferers but the God who suffers…through the prism of my tears I have seen a suffering God.

—Nicholas Welterstorff
Lament for a Son

does love us very much even though we are mired in gloom at the present time. Good memories also have a way of helping us to trust in the future, when other times of happiness will come our way.

Because our inner vision is usually quite blurred when we are filled with painful emotions, we can easily miss the good things that are a part of each day in the present. At the end of each day, no matter how miserable it may have been, we can find at least one thing we can be grateful for. We may want to write this down each evening and to look at our "gratitude list" when we are feeling particularly discouraged.

❧ *Pray your pain.* If we feel sad and empty, these feelings will naturally affect our prayer. We cannot separate ourselves from our bodies or our emotions when we pray. We need to accept the fact that we probably will not have a sense of God's presence for a while. God understands this and loves us in our humanness.

As we grieve our loss, it helps to deliberately pray our pain, to cry out to God, to express our anger. Writing a letter to God, telling God how we feel, can help us to experience being "heard" by God. We can also write a letter from God to us, noting what God would want to say to us at this time of loss.

We may also need to find other forms of prayer for a while. If we are restless, we could go for a long walk or listen to music. If our mind is constantly filled with remembrances of the loss, we could quietly repeat a scripture verse or formal prayer. If we are overwhelmed with sadness, we may find that just sitting with empty hands held open is the only prayer that we can pray. As we do so, we say with our open hands that we trust God to fill our lives with strength enough for another day.

> *"There are moments when I feel like a little bird, tucked away in a great protective Hand."*
>
> —Etty Hillisum
> *An Interrupted Life:*
> *The Diaries of Etty Hillisum, 1941-1943*

∾ *Look for God in unexpected ways.* We tend to look for God in certain familiar ways. Consequently, we may think God is absent, yet God is there in ways we may not have noticed. It may be the kindness of someone who writes us a letter or makes a phone call to see how we are. It could be the beauty of the stars on a night when we cannot sleep.

A friend of mine who was in great pain from cancer told me that during her many sleepless nights she would hear the first birdsong in the dawn. When this happened, it would lift her heart and bring her a deep sense of closeness to God.

Another woman who was in much grief told me how she looked out her window one day and saw a spider spinning a web. The threads were wet with dew and sparkled in the sunlight. As she gazed on this intricate wonder, she saw her own life woven into God's heart. This insight filled her with peace for the first time in many months.

❧ *Make time for solitude.* As difficult as it may be to take quiet time for ourselves and to be in solitude, we need to do so. We may feel terribly restless or lonely and want to run from the pain or keep ourselves very busy. But solitude is essential and necessary for our growth.

…[Job] undergoes a conversion in his mind and heart: from complaining about what he has lost to concentrating on what he is—a son of God. In the realization of his sonship he experiences the meaning of his existence, he discovers the meaning of his life…. God alone is good. Everything we have is gift. The Lord gives and the Lord takes away…. When we realize this, it is as though everything we lost comes back to us.
—Richard Rohr and
Joseph Martos
The Great Themes of Scripture

In our solitude we are like a seed buried in the darkness of the earth, all alone and waiting. It seems as though nothing is happening, but quiet growth is taking place.

A day will come when a new green shoot will come forth from the earth. A day will come when we will discover new growth, a gradual return of peace and happiness.

❧ *Be gentle, be patient.* We are in a hurry to heal, but we must be patient with ourselves. We must look for courage, resiliency, and hope in the lives of others, noticing how they have made it through their difficult journeys. If one of these persons lives nearby, we can ask that person to tell us his or her story of loss and growth.

Finding a local support group can also ease our pain. We can hear in the lives of others some of our own experiences of grief. This, too, will encourage us to be patient as we grieve.

Sometimes we expect so much of ourselves until we realize that the road we walk is a long one for other people as well.

Take Heart | When the people of the Exodus were wandering in the wilderness, they often complained that God was far from them. Yet God was as close to them as their next breath. And God constantly reassured them of this nearness. The Exodus people eventually did find a new place of freedom and peace.

The same is true for us. Through it all, God is keeping vigil over us just as God did with the Exodus community in the wilderness. It is the kind of vigil that a parent keeps with an ailing child or the nightwatch one keeps while waiting for a loved one to come home.

Etty Hillisum experienced the great loss of her family and friends' deaths in concentration camps. She walked through years of war and suffering. Amid it all, she never gave up. One day she wrote in her diary: "There will always be a small patch of sky above, and there will always be enough space to fold two hands in prayer."

Etty Hillisum held on tightly to God in her difficult times. We need to do the same, leaning on God, believing in this compassionate Presence with us. God will, indeed, stay with us on our road to restored peace and joy.

Joyce Rupp, O.S.M., is the author of Fresh Bread *and* Praying Our Good-bys.

Chapter II

Finding God in Times of Loss

ॐ

By Ruth Ellen Hasser

We were riding up the slope on a ski lift for the first run of the day, our legs dangling freely over fresh powder and evergreen treetops. The air was crisp, the sky a deep blue, and the majesty of the mountains surrounded us on every side. My friend, a self-proclaimed atheist, drew in a breath and quietly muttered in awe, "It's hard not to believe in God at a time like this!"

Years later, in the far less majestic surroundings of a sterile hospital room, another friend watched her father die a slow and painful death. Here is a man who worked hard all his life, loved his family well, and never intentionally hurt a soul. Now, he hovered somewhere between life and death, struggling for four long months.

Joan's heart was breaking as she helplessly watched her father's diminishment. She ached at his undeserved pain, and at her own loss of the Daddy she loved so deeply. Her prayers for either his healing or for a quick and peaceful death apparently unanswered, she wondered, "Where is God in all of this?"

Anyone who has experienced life comes to know the pain of loss, both great and small. From those earliest moments of emerging out of the warm, comfortable place of our mothers' wombs, to those final moments of death, we each know loss intimately. As spiritual beings, we look for answers to our questions about the meaning of such losses, and we often discover that the deeper our pain, the fewer the answers we easily find. Believing in God is much easier in the majestic mountains than in the desert valleys.

Working your way through | Loss comes to us in many forms. It may involve the death of a loved one, a way of life, or a dream. We experience loss when we leave, willingly or unwillingly, a family, a job, a friend, or a home.

Loss occurs whenever we no longer have or experience something or someone to which we have assigned great meaning. It is the absence of that which is loved or longed for.

Can God truly be present in such painful experiences? How can you find God in your loss? Here are a few ideas that may help as you walk through your own desert valley.

✎ *Accept your feelings, whatever they may be.* Most people find that they experience a wide range of feelings when undergoing a loss. Along with sadness, there may be anger, resentment, even rage. If the loss is profound or tragic, questions like "Why?" or "How can a loving God allow such a thing to happen?" are common. Some people become bitter, feeling abandoned by God or blaming God for their pain. Others simply stop believing in God altogether.

As difficult as it may be, don't run away from any of the feelings you are having at this time. Give voice to them. Talk with a friend, pastor, or counselor, join a support group, or write in a journal. Shake your fist at God, scream and cry. Set aside time to vent in a way that feels safe for you. As the feelings emerge and are expressed, you may not have any clear answers to your questions, but you will notice a change in your perspective. Your ability to accept

Emptiness has to precede fullness. Spirituality is always about letting go. Always!
—Richard Rohr, O.F.M.

your loss may be intimately linked to giving your feelings the attention they deserve. At that point, your relationship with God may come back into focus, though perhaps through a different lens.

❧ *Re-imagine God.* One thing we know about God is that what we think we know about God may be just a glimpse of who God truly is. Who is God for you? Many of us still walk around with images left over from childhood. These images of God may have worked for you for many years, but perhaps are not of much help now. Maybe you've imagined God as a Judge, a Ruler, or a Santa Claus rewarding good and punishing bad behavior. Maybe God is a Trickster, a Parent, or a Teacher who "tests our faith." If God cannot be found as you experience this loss, it is time to look to other descriptions or images of the Divine.

One place to start is the Bible. Keith McClellan, O.S.B., describes it as a record of the diverse religious experiences of many women and men, offering us a rich collage of God-pictures. "There you will find God portrayed as a walking companion, anxious parent, passionate debater, comforting mother, prodigal father, co-sufferer." Contrast your current expectations of God with the biblical experiences described in these images. Open yourself up to new possibilities of who God can be for you.

> "*Every painful event contains in itself a seed of growth and liberation.*"
> —Anthony de Mello, S.J.

❧ *Keep trying to pray.* Maybe you haven't prayed much lately, or you feel that when you have prayed, there was no noticeable response from God. Perhaps your old ways of praying are not meeting your needs as you make your way through this loss. If so, try something different. There are no rules here!

You may sing, dance, write, and cry your prayers. You may create poetry, sculpt or paint your prayers. You may want to laugh, shout, or sit quietly alone or with others to pray. You can read spiritual literature, study scripture, or attend large services at your mosque, temple, or church. Some people pray in small groups in each others' homes, while others create new prayer rituals in their own homes. You may find comfort in the prayer rituals of earlier religious training. Or, consider going on a retreat to open yourself to God in a new way during this time of loss and change.

Whatever way you choose to pray, pray for yourself and for others affected by this loss. There is no wrong way to pray when you pray from your heart. Remember that the purpose of prayer is not to change God, but to open us up so we might know God's love and desires for us.

∾ *Recall how God has loved you in the past.* In the days and weeks following my father's sudden death, God cared for me in immeasurable ways. The cards, prayers, flowers, and hugs from friends; the delicious meals cooked lovingly for me on those days I would have otherwise eaten cold cereal for dinner; the understanding of office colleagues at my frequent forgetfulness; all were evidence of God's tender mercies in my life. At the time, I was just "getting by." Looking back, God's love is crystal clear.

It is often the experience of people of faith that, although they may not recognize it at the time, God was there for them in their time of need. I often hear stories from friends or students who can see, in hindsight, how the Divine sustained them.

For I am convinced that neither death, nor life, nor angels, nor rulers, nor things present, nor things to come, nor powers, nor height, nor depth, nor anything else in all creation, will be able to separate us from the love of God....
—Romans 8: 38-39

Consider how God has loved you in your past. Begin a gratitude list of the ways you have been loved. Trust that, though hidden from your sight now, God is indeed sustaining you, even as you take your next breath.

☙ *Let go.* Veronica's loss involves the dream of birthing a baby. As her infertility becomes evident, she grieves profoundly. Each year that passes, new layers of grief are uncovered as she attends the baptism of a friend's child, wakes up to a quiet Christmas morning, or watches an office colleague grow large with child for nine months. Each time, she grieves and must let go of her dream yet again.

We all have to let go, usually again and again. If we are to heal from any loss, and to know God's presence in that loss, we must let go of that to which we cling. It may be a loved one, a job, a dream, or an ego need.

This cannot be rushed into, for letting go has its own timetable. But, finally, it must be done. As we have acknowledged our feelings, prayed our losses, and recalled God's faithfulness, we have been poured out completely.

When we let go, we make room for God to fill us in ways we could never have known before.

Take Heart | Shortly after her father died, Joan was able to reflect back and notice that, though incredibly difficult, those final months with him provided her and her family with many graces. The time together allowed them to "say once more how much we loved him, and to thank him for what he taught us. Although he was suffering, we were still able to hold his hand." She was graced with an awareness of the sacrament of time. Joan found that by embracing the mystery of his dying, and releasing her father into God's care, she was able to know a peace that "answers" alone cannot give.

So, too, with each of us. God's love and grace is available to us each moment of each day, in both our magnificent mountains and in our driest desert valleys. Sometimes, all we need is a quiet moment of prayer to recall that grace. Other times, it may come to us in the touch of a hand, the scent of fresh bed linens, the sight of the sky at daybreak, or in the loving goodbye between parent and child. We are never forgotten or forsaken. We have been carved into the palm of God's hand.

Ruth Ellen Hasser *is a writer, youth minister, and religious educator living in St. Louis, Missouri.*

CHAPTER III

When Someone's Suffering or Death Makes You Question Your Faith

෴

By Peggy Ekerdt

T ears streaming down her face, Laura sat next to me talking about her recent miscarriage. "I just don't understand it. We're good people— and wanting a baby is a good thing. I prayed so hard for this baby. Why didn't God answer my prayers?

"I've always felt like God answered my prayers before. Now I'm not sure God is listening. I'm not even sure God is there. What kind of God would let this happen?"

Working your way through	Perhaps Laura's questions are your questions, too. There are times in all of our lives when

the suffering and death of those we love force us to take a hard look at what we believe. It can be frightening to question the faith that has always been a part of our lives. But it is OK to question, so let's explore the feelings that are there.

∾ *Don't avoid the pain.* The pain will not go away if you ignore it. So do consider the questions, cry the tears, feel the anger, and express the fear. You are not losing your faith when you ask questions. Many times the questions, if you stay with them, will lead you into a deeper relationship with God. Write about what you are feeling in a journal or talk to good friends. Accept the help of those who have experienced similar losses; while no two human experiences are exactly alike, they can understand in a way that others do not. Seek the counsel of a spiritual friend or mentor.

And be patient. A colleague who has worked with hundreds of grieving families often says that there is no way out of the suffering but to simply acknowledge and walk through it. It can be hard to hear this, because we like to fix things, and fix them quickly. But there are no detours or shortcuts, so walk through the pain. As you well know, there are days when it seems that the ache in your heart will never mend. In those hard moments, believe that in time you will get to the other side of the pain.

〜 *Challenge the idea that life is perfect.* On a shelf in our living room sits a family Bible that is my personal reminder that suffering is certainly not new, nor is life fair. This Bible contains a record of family births and deaths. Under deaths, there is this grim series of entries: *Hanora died October 16, 1878; Mary died October 17, 1878; Margret died October 17, 1878; Josephine died October 19, 1878; Gertrude died October 28, 1878.*

In 12 days time, my great-grandparents, Andrew and Sarah Harty, buried five of their eight young daughters, ages 11 to 1. The entry does not stop here. Andrew adds the death of another daughter, Laura, in 1884, and then this: "Sarah Harty, my beloved wife, died July 28, 1886 after a painful illness of five weeks. May Almighty God have mercy on her eternal soul."

We are bombarded with cultural messages that showcase perfection as a worthy and attainable goal. But we know it just isn't so. Whether we like it or not, suffering is an unavoidable part of life. We don't have to look

> *There are places in the heart which do not yet exist, and into them suffering enters so that they may have existence.*
> —Leon Bloy

far to recognize that. We all know families who have buried children; we have brave friends who fight cancer. There are people who starve to death each day in our world, and others who battle addiction to no avail. Yet, while we all know that suffering is a part of life, when it becomes our own personal suffering, it somehow seems singularly unfair.

Those Bible entries, in my great-grandfather's hand, are his legacy to me and mine: Suffering is a part of life—yet in the midst of suffering, God is still with us.

❧ *Reexamine your image of God.* God may be with us, but like my friend Laura, we may sometimes find it hard to believe. Perhaps we need to think about how we understand God. As children we were encouraged to pray, but little was actually said about the God who hears our prayers. We may have been told about God the eternal, all-powerful Creator, but little else was disclosed.

For some of us, lacking further details, God became something like a magical jukebox—deposit a coin (your prayer) and get your request. Ask to win the game, get into the college of choice, find the perfect spouse, sell the house, cure the illness, close the deal—ask and God will grant the request. True, Jesus did say, "Seek, and you will find" (Matthew 7:7 and Luke 11:9). But he did not say *seek whatever you want* and God will provide. What I believe Jesus was actually telling us was this: Seek my kingdom and you will find justice and peace. Keep looking, and a door will open to show you the way.

"Doubt is but another element of faith."
—Saint Augustine

When suffering occurs and God does not seem to answer our prayers, we can either walk away or look and listen more closely to find God. It is true that it is not possible to know God completely on this side of life. God is mystery and beyond our understanding, for God's ways are not our ways (Isaiah 55:8). Yet it is equally true that God wants to be in relationship with each one of us and will be made known to us, bit by bit, if we but pay attention.

We know God in the love of other human beings—for God is love—and though we have never seen the face of God, God is present when we love (1 John 4). Gracious, merciful, and abounding in steadfast love (Psalms 145 and 25), God formed us in our mothers' wombs and knows our innermost thoughts (Psalm 139). God is near to all who call, and is a rock, a refuge, and a source of strength (Psalms 18, 62, and 144). God keeps count of our tears (Psalm 56) and if we pay careful attention, God will show us the path of life (Psalm 16). God, who watched his own son suffer and cry out in abandonment (Matthew 27:46), is nonetheless a God of consolation who consoles us in our affliction (2 Corinthians 1:6) and promises that we will never be abandoned (John 14). How could this God not stand with us in our suffering and pain?

Life is not perfect or fair. If it were, would we recognize joy when we experienced it? Easter only has meaning because of the suffering and loss that came on Good Friday. It is mystery—but it is our life. And in the joy and in the pain, God loves us with an everlasting love and faithfulness that never ends (Jeremiah 31:3).

❧ *Suffering can have redeeming value.* After

To each one of us Christ is saying: If you want your life and mission to be fruitful like mine, do as I. Be converted into a seed that lets itself be buried. . . Do not be afraid. Those who shun suffering will remain alone. No one is more alone than the selfish. But if you give your life out of love for others, as I give mine for all, you will reap a great harvest.
—Archbishop Oscar Arnulfo Romero
The Violence of Love

years of infertility, we conceived and prepared for the birth of our first child. After some hours of labor, we made the drive to the local hospital. As we entered the birthing room, I remember feeling afraid of the pain and of the unknown.

I was 30 years old, had a great husband/coach by my side, and we were, if anything, over-prepared for childbirth. But I was still nervous and fearful. The nurses told us that there was only one other woman in labor—a 16-year-old girl who was all alone. The stark contrast was not lost on me.

As I labored through the night—and on occasion heard that young woman cry out in pain—I remember wishing that she was not alone, offering my own pain for her. It sounds kind of corny as I write it now, but it is a vivid memory. I have always believed that my prayer for her eased my own pain.

Although it is difficult to explain, there are many who say that their suffering is made bearable by the belief that, offered on behalf of others, suffering is a source of grace and transformation. There are times, quite frankly, when those words scare me, for who wants to open the door to suffering? At the same time, my birthing-room experience was a story of grace in my own life that makes me a believer.

Take Heart | It is obvious that the pain of childbirth brings forth life. The pain and suffering of terminal illness does not seem to have such a reward. But if we believe that we were created for eternal life, and that death is simply the crossing from one life to another, then suffering does lead to life. It is not a view of suffering that is often espoused. It is, however, at the center of Christian faith. From death and suffering come life.

One of my favorite hymns, *Pues Si Vivimos/If We Are Living*, has a simple haunting melody, with these words: "If we are living, we are in the Lord, and if we die, we are in the Lord. For if we live or if we die, we belong to God, we belong to God." These words can serve as a reminder to all of us that, no matter what, we do belong to God, and we are never alone.

Peggy Ekerdt is a pastoral associate and spiritual director at Visitation Church in Kansas City, Missouri. She is married to David Ekerdt and the mother of two twentysomething daughters.

CHAPTER IV

Five Key Beliefs to Get You Through a Loss

∽

By Carol Luebering

When he was in college, my nephew Tom worked in a hospital laundry. One day the brake on the spin-dryer wasn't working. Rather than wait for the drum to coast to a stop, Tom did something a lesser man could not have done (he is 6'8"). He put his foot atop the inner lid and applied pressure. That worked fine for a while, but then the lid slipped and his foot went in. The spinning drum twisted his leg and tore the major artery in his leg.

Thanks to the quick thinking of his younger brother, who was working beside him, and the nearness of the emergency room, he didn't bleed to death. He didn't even go into shock. But the loss of circulation to his lower leg caused major tissue damage. One year and several surgeries later, the only option left was to amputate his leg just below the knee.

Whatever your loss, it has left you just as far from whole. Like an upset canoer, you find yourself being swept where you never wanted to go, and looking desperately for something to hold onto. This chapter will place a few strong branches within your reach.

Working your way through | Any significant loss takes part of our self with it. Perhaps that's most obvious when a death strips us of someone who was in a real way a part of us, but it's also true of divorce, moving from a well-loved home, losing a job, or retiring from a career.

Furthermore, a painful loss pulls the solid earth out from under our feet. Every certainty we have ever held is suddenly open to question. We no longer know what to believe. If you can manage to accept the following five truths, they will help you get through this awful time.

❧ *You will survive.* This is true not because you are strong or brave or wise—attributes you may feel lacking right now. You will survive simply because that's the nature of being human.

The world is full of people who have come through horrendous experiences and still managed to get on with life. Think of the people who survived the Nazi death camps. They lost *everything*: home, livelihood, family, human dignity; yet they were able to start all over again.

Today, Tom is a busy executive, a loving husband, and the proud father of three teens. I stopped worrying about him long ago—the summer after he lost his leg. That was when he ordered a new artificial one that strapped on more securely so he could play pick-up basketball with his friends. I knew then that he would lead a full life in spite of losing a part of himself. And so can you.

Like my nephew, you will never again be quite the same as you were before the loss. Your loss will remain unrecovered for the rest of your life. But you will walk tall again— even run!

Getting to that point won't be a stroll in the park. But you will discover strength

> *Grief work in many ways is not unlike childbirth—both are painful, but both, when carried through successfully, can bring forth something worthwhile. There is no way to escape the suffering of grief any more than there is to escape the pain that follows surgery or severe disease. . . . Grief, too, is an illness, a wound that heals slowly, often erratically, and always painfully.*
> —Arthur Freese
> *Help for Your Grief*

you never dreamed possible. You will become more sensitive to other people's pain, and better able to express your compassion in helpful ways because you will have learned what helps and what doesn't. (It's no coincidence that a multitude of programs from Alcoholics Anonymous to Mothers Against Drunk Driving owe their existence to folks who have *been there*.) But first you have a journey ahead of you.

❧ *You have a right to grieve.* Well-meaning people may try to talk you out of your grief. But grief is a feeling—more precisely, a pot full of feelings that keep boiling over: sorrow, numbness, anger, guilt, depression. Feelings just don't respond to logic because they rise from your heart, not your head.

Grieving is a process you go through, just as you would go through physical therapy after a crippling injury. And, as my 93-year-old aunt says of her remarkable recovery from a badly broken hip, "I worked very hard for a long and painful time." Grieving requires working through the pain—owning the feelings and struggling with them until they carry you toward healing. Healing doesn't mean forgetting your loss. You never will. Rather, healing enables you to accept it as a part of your life and move on.

❧ *You don't have to go it alone.* Nor should you. God doesn't pass out "get out of grief free" cards. God gives us something even better: each other. Ever since Abraham packed up his family and belongings to make a long trip across a desert at God's call, that same God has depended on human agents.

"Healing doesn't mean forgetting your loss. You never will. Rather, healing enables you to accept it as a part of your life and move on."

Of course no one knows exactly how you feel. Your loss is unique. Yet it has much in common with other experiences of loss. Support groups for people who have lost health or a loved one abound, and many people find comfort in being with others who truly understand their pain. Your own circle of acquaintances includes people who have made it through trying times; seek them out. Ask your faith community for the support of their prayers and any practical assistance you can use. Ask your clergy to put you in touch with survivors of a loss similar to yours.

In others who have suffered loss, you will find understanding ears, soft shoulders, and practical advice on matters large and small. ("Cry in the shower," one widow advised another, "and your eyes won't get puffy.")

🙠 *God is good.* Don't forget to seek God's company. Pray—even if all you can do is scream. God is close to the brokenhearted, scripture promises. Tender as a mother, God says little but holds us tight in silent promise that everything *will* be all right.

There is a persistent rumor that God sends suffering our way for some good but unexplained reason. That rumor contradicts everything we know about the biblical God. The prophet Isaiah described this God as a gracious host who not only invites us to a great banquet, but also wipes the tears from the guests' faces so that they can enter fully into the festivities (see Isaiah 25:6-8).

Believing that God is good doesn't mean you can't shake your fist at heaven. Unlike people who you might yell at in your pain without warning, God is neither surprised nor shocked at your anger, and God is big enough to take it. Follow the example of Job, who complained to God at great length that his suffering wasn't fair.

Life is a gift to be enjoyed, not just endured…. Grieving is a way…back to the enjoyment of this cherished gift….
—Alla Bozarth-Campbell
Life Is Goodbye, Life Is Hello

☙ *Love never goes to waste.* Of the many losses we face, the ones that really hurt are losses of people and things we have dearly loved. Love makes us vulnerable. It also strengthens us. According to the Song of Songs, love is as strong as death (see 8:6-7).

Everything we have cherished remains part of us even when times are dark. No one can take away the experiences, the things you have learned. Your happy memories are yours to keep. A young man whose toddler had died put it this way: "She was such a joy. I wouldn't for a minute trade having had her for relief from all this pain."

Take Heart | My home is furnished with antiques, mostly "early Goodwill" pieces I have refinished. I never try to remove all the scars. These pieces have a history; I don't want them to look like they just came from the manufacturer's showroom. The same is true of us. Who we are is shaped by our history, by our scars no less than by our triumphs.

Every spring brings the solemn observances of Passover and Easter. At the Seder meal, Jews keep alive the memory of their suffering in Egypt and celebrate their deliverance. The ritual includes a gracious gesture of solidarity with all who suffer: Ten drops of wine are poured out in memory of the pain their freedom cost the Egyptians. Christian depictions of their risen Lord show the wounds in his hands and feet. With believing people all over the world, trust that the God who has delivered others will indeed deliver you from your grief, as you journey the path to new life.

Carol Luebering, *freelance writer and retired editor, is a frequent CareNotes contributor. Her books include* When You Are a Grandparent *and four other titles in the "Handing on the Faith" series from St. Anthony Messenger Press, and* Called to Marriage *and* A Retreat with Job and Julian of Norwich, *from the same publisher.*

CHAPTER V

Healing Your Grief Through Prayer and Meditation

∾

By Linus Mundy

When someone we love dies, many of us turn inward for time alone with our sorrow. Others draw closer to friends and family for consolation and company. Still others look inward, outward—and *"upward"*—for help and hope. This chapter is written to encourage this last option. Grieving folks need help, after all, from every direction it may come.

As I write this, I am grieving the death of a good friend, and I realize that you may be experiencing grief perhaps more devastating than mine—the death of a parent, a spouse, a child, or other close family member. But grief by any name is still grief. With the loss of my friend Pat, I find myself turning in many directions seeking consolation and hope. And one of those directions is "up." Pat would want it that way. And at times of pain and loss all major faith traditions send us, I think, a personal invitation to look all around—and up.

Working your way through | When we're confronting a profound loss, our concern for spiritual issues can reach a peak, no matter our religious orientation. When we're being swallowed up by the waves of grief, we find ourselves turning to our faith tradition, or at least grappling with it. Says grief author Ken Doka, "Grief pulls the rug out from under us and leaves us saying, 'Wait a minute, I have to check this. I believed this and this and so and so, and now I'm not so sure.'"

The task becomes one of "reconstructing meaning." And prayer and meditation can help. Indeed, there are many prayer forms to help us on our healing journey—ranging from private prayer to community prayer to sitting and waiting and listening.

Here are some ways to stretch our understanding of the practices of prayer and meditation in times of grief and loss.

꙳ *Let God pray for you.* Religion writer Martin Marty recounts how his doubting daughter once told him that she just "wasn't the believing type." He countered her by saying, "Don't worry about it; God believes in you."

We can all be grateful for that kind of support, since sometimes after loss, faith and prayer may not come easily. Crying and being angry and in pain seem to come so much more readily. The key is to see these emotions as prayers themselves.

Mauryeen O'Brien writes in *Praying Through Grief*, "Because death forces us to assess our spiritual lives, the struggle with our grief can help God enter into daily existence. The hurts and wounds caused by our loss give God a chance to enter in." If you, like many, are experiencing anger at God for taking someone you love, or "allowing" your loved one to die, prayer lets you express that anger. You may really be asking, "God, where were you?!"—or you may even be ready to

Prayer and ritual will also be an important part of our healing process in our journey through grief....If we commemorate and celebrate birth and marriage, parenthood and ordination, why not do the same as we face the death of our loved ones, gathering together the memories that made them so special to us?
—Mauryeen O'Brien
Praying Through Grief

"have a fight" with God in prayer, as one acquaintance did, who went into a church shouting to God: "Let's have it out."

Sometimes we need to pray (ask God) for faith itself—for answers to our questions and guidance for our doubts—especially when we are vexed by God's action (or apparent inaction!). And we need to pray all of our emotions, not just the "sweet ones."

∾ *Expand your definition of prayer and meditation.* Earlier I talked about turning "inward," "outward," and "upward." But God isn't just "up there"; and we aren't just "down here." Instead, we and God are "in this mess together." God is right here in the thick of all this grief with us.

Prayer and meditation connect us to the love of God, and they can bring us closer to God. But they help us the most, I think, by helping us see ourselves—and the loved one(s) we have lost—as spiritual beings. Through the eyes of faith we see ourselves as spiritual travelers on the way home. And once we recognize that, we see that the gift of faith can bring peace and meaning to our world of sorrow and uncertainty like no other gift can.

When death and tragedy strike, we have an innate need to try to explain it, to give it meaning. Prayer and meditation bring our hearts and souls into the spiritual realm, which is perhaps the only realm where meaning can be found—and transcended. To paraphrase Rabbi Harold S. Kushner: If logic doesn't help you explain God or God's ways, don't give up on God; give up on logic. When someone we love dies, we are invited into the mystery—whether we want the invitation or not. And mysteries defy logic. Getting to God's level, getting the "God's-eye-view" of death and life, allows us to transcend the pain, to pass from grief to grace.

"Our grief puts us to the spiritual test—and trusting that God's healing power will intervene in our lives may be one of the most difficult things we ever do."

✎ *Pray for your loved one—and yourself.* Do you know it's OK to pray for yourself? As a matter of fact, there may be no more important reason to pray. Pray for hope. Pray for the strength, the will, to get out of bed in the morning, the strength to find your way after the death of someone you now miss so much.

And praying for your loved one is also healing. As one child said, "Since my brother died, my friends think he's not my brother anymore. But he is. I still talk to him." Talking to God about your loved one is no less than prayer, and no less than what a loving God would expect.

In time there can even be joy in our prayers for a loved one. "Joy is possible in grief," says Father John Catoir, "because joy is not the absence of pain, joy is the presence of God's life within us." When we pray for our loved one, we put God's life-giving presence into the picture with us and our loved one.

ᴥ *Explore the healing power of meditation.* Whether we call it *meditation* or *contemplation* or something else, this practice is one wherein we quiet the mind and simply invite the Divine to be present with us. And who better to accompany us in this trying time? Feeling God's care and nearness to us can bring the utmost healing benefit.

But just how do we "do" meditation or contemplation? One of the best responses I've ever heard is: "It doesn't much

Prayer is not a stratagem for occasional use, a refuge to resort to now and then. It is rather like an established residence for the innermost self. All things have a home; the bird has a nest, the fox has a hole, the bee has a hive. A soul without prayer is a soul without a home.
—Abraham Joshua Heschel

matter as long as you leave something for God to do." Said another wise practitioner: "Do it your way—the way you think it should be done. If you don't know how to be a contemplative, be what a 'contemplative' means to you."

Most of all, meditation helps us realize that maybe we are doing too much thinking. Maybe we have an internal "chatter machine" running, as we think the same thoughts over and over, busily trying to come up with solutions and answers. Meditation stills the mind and shuts off the stream of thoughts that keep us from seeing things as a whole. To meditate well is to surrender to God, and the ability to do that takes practice.

Meditation means giving oneself a time and place for deep reflection. When we're grieving, it gives us a time, place, and technique for acknowledging our loss at the very core of our being—in "that quiet space, that place of depth and meaning where God dwells," as Mauryeen O'Brien says in *Praying Through Grief.*

Take Heart | In our mourning, we may have a multitude of words to say—or very little. We may choose, as our best prayer, to sit in quiet meditation, resting in the presence of God. And, in time, God will speak peace and consolation and hope to us. God blesses and comforts all who mourn.

I once heard a person who had just lost a loved one say, in all sincerity, "It will take a miracle for me to get through this." The truth is, that's what it takes for any of us to survive, isn't it? Sometimes only God can get us through.

Linus Mundy has written a number of books for children and grown-ups, as well as articles for the religious press. The founder of the popular CareNotes and CareNotes for Kids booklet series from Abbey Press, he has written *Slow-down Therapy* and *Keep-life-simple Therapy*, and several books on prayer and spiritual growth. Linus and his wife, Michaelene, wrote the *Bringing Religion Home* newsletter for a number of years.